GOOGLE PIXEL

8 AND 8 PRO

USER GUIDE

The Complete Step-By-Step Manual To Help Both Beginners & Seniors Master The Google Pixel 8 And 8 Pro With The Aid Of Pictures & Tips & Tricks For Android 14

BY

Williams M. Brown

Table Of Contents

INTRODUCTION

Google has unveiled two new smartphones, the Pixel 8 and the Pixel 8 Pro, that emphasize artificial intelligence to provide a better and more personalized user experience. With the help of Google Tensor G3, each of these phones offers capabilities that no other smartphone has. Their device will be eligible for seven years of free Android OS upgrades, security fixes, and feature drops. Pay close attention to the new phones' unique sensors, enhanced cameras, and expertly crafted bodies as you investigate them further.

A Polished Look Made For Your Everyday

With its refined aesthetic, softer edges, stunning metal accents, and eco-friendly materials, the Pixel 8 and Pixel 8 Pro are perfect for daily use.

The smaller Pixel 8 and its rounded edges make it a pleasure to hold. The 6.2-inch Actua display is 42% brighter than the Pixel 7's and provides real-world clarity. The Pixel 8 is available in Rose, Hazel, and Obsidian, and it has a polished glass rear, satin metal accents, and a metal body.

The 6.7-inch Super Actua display on the Pixel 8 Pro is our brightest one to date. You will be pleasantly surprised by how accurate your Ultra HDR photos seem, even when shot in bright sunshine. It is available in three different colors—Porcelain, Bay, and Obsidian—and has a polished aluminum frame with a matte glass back.

A new temperature sensor, located on the rear of the Pixel 8 Pro, allows you to swiftly scan an item to get its temperature. You may use it to see if the milk in your baby's bottle is at the correct temperature or to see whether the pan is hot enough to begin cooking. Additionally, we have applied to the FDA to allow the Pixel Thermometer app to record your temperature and send it to Fitbit.

More Advancements In The Camera

Superior image and video capture and groundbreaking editing tools are standard on both the Pixel 8 and the Pixel 8 Pro, thanks to their cutting-edge camera systems.

The Pixel 8 Pro's main camera is only the beginning of its improved camera system, which improves low-light photography and video recording across the board. Improved Macro Focus from the larger ultrawide lens, 56% more light captured by the telephoto lens, 10x optical quality photographs taken by the front-facing camera, and autofocus for the finest selfies ever on a Pixel phone—all thanks to these upgrades.

In addition to the upgraded primary camera, the Pixel 8 now has an ultrawide lens that supports Macro Focus.

You can now access your preferred picture and video modes with ease thanks to the new and user-friendly camera app. On top of that, the Pixel 8 Pro has Pro Controls that let you tweak the Pixel Camera's artistic features. These controls include things like shutter speed, ISO, and the ability to take 50 MP photographs at any magnification level, among other things.

It's happened to all of us: just when you thought you had the ideal group shot, someone starts to look away. You may acquire the snapshot you imagined taking with Best Take1 by using the photographs you took. To do this, an algorithm running on the smartphone combines many photographs to get the greatest possible appearance for each user.

With the new experimental editing experience called Magic Editor in Google images, you can utilize generative AI to make your images more true to the moment you were attempting to capture. Subjects may be easily resized and moved with a few clicks, and you can even utilize presets to make the backdrop stand out.

You may use Audio Magic Eraser1 to swiftly and efficiently erase distracting sounds from your video, such as wind noise or a huge crowd. This revolutionary computational audio feature sorts sounds into separate layers so you may regulate their volumes using sophisticated machine learning algorithms.

Video Boost, which integrates Tensor G3 with our powerful data centers, will be available to Pixel 8 Pro customers later this year, giving them access to cutting-edge video processing. It creates breathtaking, photorealistic films by adjusting brightness, contrast, saturation, stabilization, and graininess. Night Sight Video, which improves smartphone video quality in low light, is also enabled via Video Boost on Pixel.

Tools That Enhance Efficiency And Productivity

More context and page depth are now at your fingertips. To help you grasp the main ideas of a site fast, Pixel has a feature called Summarise. Plus, your Pixel can translate websites and read aloud, so you can listen to content while you're on the road.2

If you want to get things done more organically, you can chat with Pixel as it understands human speech subtleties even better. By just pausing or saying "um," it will patiently wait for you to finish speaking before reacting. If you speak more than one language, you may still use your voice to swiftly compose, modify, and send messages.

Call Screen has improved its AI to the point where it cuts spam calls in half on average.3 It can subtly interact with unknown callers by using a voice that seems more human. Additionally, it has the intelligence to distinguish between the calls you want and those you do not. You may soon react to basic calls, like appointment confirmations, without answering the phone by tapping on contextual answers suggested by Call Screen.

7 Years Of Updates To Keep You And Your Personal Information Secure

Google Tensor G3 and the Titan M2 security chip work together to make the Pixel more resistant to sophisticated attacks and better safeguard private information. The Pixel 8's Face Unlock meets the most stringent Android biometric standards, allowing you to utilize Google Wallet and other compatible banking and payment apps.

As time goes by, your Pixel phone will continue to improve thanks to the special features and upgrades you get. Our Pixel 8 and Pixel 8 Pro will be supported by software upgrades, security patches, and regular feature drops for seven years. This is a first for our phone lineup.

THE NEW FEATURES OF THE GOOGLE PIXEL 8 AND 8 PRO

The new Pixel phones are fantastic for many reasons, but here are a few to get you started:

1. 7 Years Of Operating System Updates, Security Patches, And Feature Drops

The Pixel continues to get better with each update, and now Google is extending support for the Pixel to seven years of security patches, Android OS upgrades, feature drops, and advancements in generative artificial intelligence for phones.2 Support for the Pixel 8 and Pixel 8 Pro will continue until 2030. This kind of dedicated support and endurance is unmatched by any other major smartphone maker. Since they will be maintained for seven years, these phones are a sustainable and long-lasting decision.

2. Audio Magic Eraser And Video Boost Bring Out The Sounds And Visuals You Want While Cutting The Noise

You almost got the ideal video of your joyful, screaming kid at the park, but the audio was spoiled by the roaring wind. Fortunately, Audio Magic Eraser on Pixel makes it simple to lower annoying background noise in videos by sorting sounds into separate layers and letting you adjust their volume. Visually, it's better as well. Pixel 8 Pro users may take advantage of Video Boost, a feature included in the December Feature Drop, which enhances video processing by automatically adjusting lighting, color, stabilization, and graininess.

3. Google Assistant Summarize And Voice Typing Will Speed Up Your Reading And Writing

When time is of the essence but you still need to get the gist of a long piece, Google Assistant Summarise is a godsend. With a single press on the "summarise" button, your Pixel will provide you with a concise summary. Voice typing also doubles the speed of message writing, and you can use Google Assistant to have websites read aloud or translated so you can listen to content while you're on the road.

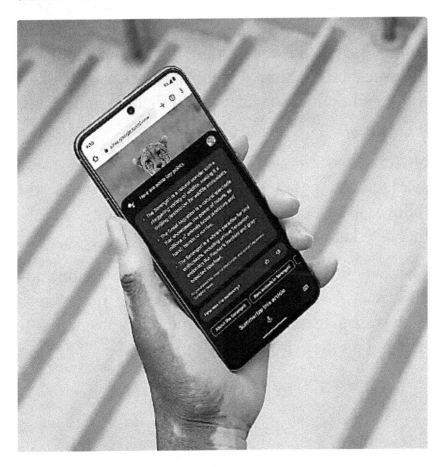

4. Assistant With Bard Is A Personal Helper In Your Pocket

Incorporating reasoning, generative capabilities, and personalized support, the generative AI phone conversation tool Bard is joining Google Assistant. So, it can hear, talk, and see, and it can even conduct useful things like creating a shopping list for a weekend get-together with friends who have different dietary needs—all from the ease of your always-on device.4 Spoken English request: "Could you please provide a shopping list for ten people for the weekend?" "Supply a lot of snacks; we'll likely want a smoothie, so suggest and include ingredients for that."

Note: Assistant with Bard will soon be made available to a small group of testers. Over the following several months, the availability will be increased as an opt-in experience.

The benefits of owning a Google Pixel phone are always evolving, with each generation introducing even more useful features and enhancements to existing phones via software upgrades.

5. Class 3 Face Unlock

Most high-end Android phones include a face unlock feature. However, its use is restricted to unlocking the device. Most phones' biometric verification methods aren't safe enough to utilize for banking app access, payment authorization, and other sensitive tasks. Both the Pixel 8 and the Pixel 8 Pro include Class 3 Face Unlock, which is the "highest Android biometric class." Face unlock is now compatible with payment applications and other apps that need biometric identification, providing an extra layer of security.

Impressive, really, since Google managed to pull it off with only the new 10.5MP selfie cameras on the Pixel 8 series. The Pixel 4 was the final Google phone to have this feature, however, it came with its own set of hardware. To provide a safe identification experience, even Apple's Face ID on the iPhone uses extra sensors.

Nevertheless, Google has accomplished this by using the AI and machine learning algorithms included within the Titan M2 processor and Tensor G3. Because of this, it's very doubtful that the functionality will be available on the Pixel 6 and 7 series.

6. Magic Editor

Consider Magic Eraser a miraculous product. Hold off till you give Magic Editor a go. Uses "semantic understanding and generative AI" to allow you to rearrange a subject in your shot, first presented by Google at I/O 2023. Change the sky's tone, brightness, cloudiness, and more with this handy tool. To be fair, you probably already have these capabilities in Photoshop or any other high-end picture editor. On the other hand, the Magic Editor puts all of this power in your hands, readily usable with a few touches on the Pixel 8 series.

Google may port Magic Editor to additional Android and iOS devices in the future, as it is an extension of

Magic Eraser. However, at this time, a Pixel 8 is required to test out Magic Editor. By using the on-device AI, the Pixel 8's Magic Eraser can remove more complex and wider areas of photographs with fewer artifacts.

7. Magic Eraser For Audio

On the Pixel 8, you can use Google's AI Magic for more than just images and movies. Another option is the Magic Audio Eraser, which promises to eliminate distracting audio from your films. According to Google, the function can detect common sounds like wind, music, and background conversations by using sophisticated ML models. After then, they're broken down into many layers that you may tweak separately to suit your demands.

8. Enhance Video

Google has put a lot of focus on the Pixel 8's photography skills this year, with the inclusion of several new features driven by AI. One Pixel 8 Pro-exclusive upgrade, Video Boost, would supposedly improve recorded movies' dynamic range, colors, and textures. Use Night Sight Video if you're in a low-light situation.

Both of these improvements will be accessible in the December update, but they won't be available when the Pixel 8 Pro launches. Regardless, Google's presentation is promising. We wonder whether the Tensor G3 processor makes a difference since Video Boost is so resource-intensive that it depends on Google's cloud servers to provide the final output.

There may be other flagship phones with higher video capturing capabilities than the Pixel 8 Pro, such as the Samsung Galaxy S23 Ultra, but none of them include a feature like Video Boost to enhance the captured footage even more. Including the base model Pixel 8, this is something that is missing.

9. Best Take

Whether you're a fan of group photographs or not, Best Take says it will be a breeze. Taking several photos and then using Best Take to combine the faces is all it takes to obtain the perfect group portrait. The best thing about Best Take is how easy it is to use. Although there are phones with superior cameras to the Pixel 8, none of them has a function that makes capturing group shots a breeze. No longer will you have to hold your breath for everyone to have their finest smiles before taking a picture.

10.   Zoom Enhance

The Google Pixel 8 Pro can only zoom up to 30x, but the Samsung Galaxy S23 Ultra can zoom up to 100x. Zoom Enhance, however, will be standard on Google's flagship Pixel smartphone.

This feature makes use of generative AI to provide a mobile Zoom experience that is second to none. You can refocus on the part of the screen you want to focus on because, as Google puts it, the feature "intelligently fills in the gaps between pixels and predicts fine details" using generative AI.

With the video capabilities, the Pixel 8 series will be the first to get Zoom Enhance in an upcoming Pixel Feature Drop.

CHAPTER ONE

HOW TO TURN ON/OFF YOUR DEVICE

You must enter your SIM card into your phone before it may turn on.

1. Turn On Your Phone

To power on your phone, press and hold the side key.

2. Input Your PIN.

When prompted, enter your PIN and then push the right arrow button.

Entering the incorrect PIN three times in a row will deactivate the SIM. Unlocking your SIM requires entering your PUK code. Dialing 191 from a Vodafone mobile phone will bring you the PUK. From a landline, dial **03333 040 191**. Never forget that entering the wrong PUK code more than once may permanently deactivate your SIM. In this case, a new SIM card from Vodafone is required.

3. Put Your Phone To Sleep.

Depress the screen's upper corner with two fingers and drag them downward.

4. Put Your Phone To Sleep.

Choose the "Power Off" button.

5. Put Your Phone To Sleep.

Simply press the power button to disable the power.

HOW TO ACTIVATE THE SIM ON YOUR GOOGLE PIXEL 8 SERIES

Electronic SIM cards are compatible with the Google Pixel 8 and 8 Pro. Nevertheless, compared to the time-tested procedure of inserting a conventional SIM card into your phone, activating your eSIM is more involved. There has been no change to the user experience, even though eSIM support for Pixel phones has been there for a while. If you own an older Pixel phone and would want to activate or transfer an eSIM to your Pixel 8, you may do so by following this process.

These procedures are compatible with the three main US carriers as well as with smaller carriers' less expensive data plans. If you're not satisfied with your experience with the Pixel, you may simply transfer your SIM card to another device that supports eSIM since many other Android phones are also compatible.

What You Need To Activate Your eSIM

With the eSIM compatibility of the Google Pixel 8 and Pixel 8 Pro, all that's needed is the device. Where to purchase this updated version of the classic SIM card can be a mystery to those who aren't acquainted with it.

Just connect your Pixel 8 to a Wi-Fi network— something we'll get into later on—if you purchased an eSIM with your purchase.

Your carrier should give you a QR code with your eSIM to the email address linked to your account if you already own a Pixel 8. Before you start, make sure you have this QR code by contacting your carrier.

HOW TO ACTIVATE THE ESIM ON YOUR GOOGLE PIXEL 8

Enable your eSim during the Google Pixel 8 setup process. You won't have to reset your Pixel 8 if you decide to activate it later or have any issues. Follow the on-screen prompts to activate your eSim when you've finished setting it up.

Activate An eSIM During The Set Up Process

After linking your phone to Wi-Fi, you may be asked to join your carrier's network if you purchased an item from the same provider as your phone. Typically, this method takes about five minutes to get an eSIM profile.

Following the steps below will let you manually find your eSIM if it is not already there.

Activate An eSIM After Your Phone Is Set Up

This method may activate an eSIM whenever you want, regardless of whether you're a Pixel 8 newbie or just switching. All it takes is a simple QR code that your carrier provides. Kindly get in touch with your carrier's customer service department if you are unable to discover a QR code.

Advice: If you have a Pixel phone, you may scan the QR code using the camera app to avoid most of these steps. You will see the page that confirms the download.

1. Launch the Settings app on your Pixel 8.
2. Choose Network and Internet.
3. Select SIMs.

Settings

Q Search settings

🛜 **Network and Internet**
Mobile, Wi-Fi, hotspot

📠 **Connected devices**
Bluetooth, pairing

⠿ **Apps**
Assistant, recent apps, default apps

🔔 **Notifications**
Notification history, conversations

🔋 **Battery**
82% - Until 10:45

☰ **Storage**
47% used – 68.28 GB free

🔊 **Sound and vibration**
Volume, haptics, Do Not Disturb

←

Network and Internet

▼ **Internet**
SKYB8BW4

📞 **Calls and SMS**
Vodafone

🔳 **SIMs**
Vodafone

✈ Aeroplane mode

◉ **Hotspot and tethering**
Off

⟳ **Data Saver**
Off

⛏ **VPN**
None

Private DNS
Automatic

Adaptive connectivity

4. Select the "Add SIM" option.

5. Select File > Download eSIM.

Connect to mobile network

To add another SIM, download a new eSIM.

To use a different SIM card, first remove the one that's currently in your phone. Learn how to use a SIM card

Download a new eSIM

Cancel

←

SIMs

 Vodafone
Active / Default for mobile data, calls, SMS

+   Add SIM

6. Take a look at the QR code that came with your phone plan.

Scan QR code from network

If your network provider gave you a QR code, scan it now by keeping the code centred in the box

Need help?

7. To verify your eSIM, go to the bottom right of your screen and press on Download.

In about five minutes, your eSIM will be downloaded. Your Pixel phone will connect to your carrier's network immediately after the download is complete.

HOW TO MIGRATE N EXISTING ESIM TO YOUR GOOGLE PIXEL 8 SERIES

Transferring your eSIM straight from an earlier Pixel phone to a newer Pixel 8 or Pixel 8 Pro eliminates the need to manually deactivate and reactivate it. The only Pixel 8 phone that supports eSIM transfers is the Pixel 8, although any Pixel phone that supports eSIM transfers may be used.

Note: As you set up your brand new Pixel 8 phone, this choice will emerge.

After you've set up the Pixel 8, turn off the eSIM on your old phone and put the new one in. Get in touch with your service provider if you need help with this.

HOW TO ACTIVATE AN ESIM ALONGSIDE A SIMCARD IN THE PIXEL 8 SERIES

Follow these instructions to activate an eSIM in your Pixel 8 if it already has a SIM card installed.

With this feature, you may use the same phone with two different SIM cards.

The majority of service providers allow you to utilize several eSIMs simultaneously. Nevertheless, this feature could be limited by some carriers. Alternatively, you may save many eSIM profiles and then utilize just one of them.

Tip: Navigate to the SIMs section in the Settings app of your Pixel 8 to change the SIM profile.

Does eSIM Activation Vary Per Carrier?

Yes. The process of activating an eSIM is different for each phone and carrier, however it is becoming more widely available. If you're having trouble activating an eSIM on any of the three main US carriers—Verizon, T-Mobile, and AT&T—follow our instructions on how to do it with your Pixel 8 or Pixel 8 Pro.

If you're still confused, call your service provider. They can remotely activate it or even just show you the process. To download and activate your eSIM, you may have to go to a shop that your carrier has.

CHAPTER TWO

HOW TO MOVE YOUR DATA TO A PIXEL PHONE

Get the Quick Switch Adapter that comes with your Pixel phone and make sure both devices are charged to 80%. It resembles the optical thumb drive seen above.

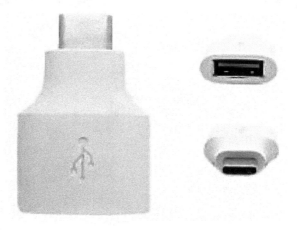

Please ensure that both phones are placed on a level surface throughout the whole process since this is a physical connection that is kept in place by two cables. This guarantees that the data flow is constant and that you won't need to have the phones in your hands the whole time.

Let's Get Started

To finish the setup process, go to your settings page and look for the green button.

Next, tap the Start button.

Go to your previous phone started, unlock it, and check that you can go to the home screen. Join the wire to the device's charging socket. After you've connected it, tap Next.

Now, plug in the Quick Switch Adapter to your Pixel. You may attach the other end of your previous phone cord to the rectangular end that is located at the bottom.

Press the Next button once you've linked both phones using the Quick Switch Adapter.

Locate your previous phone, press Copy, and then follow the on-screen prompts. You should check that the phone can still be unlocked and that it can reach the home screen completely.

You may choose whatever data from your old phone to import onto your new Pixel phone by returning it. Select the text or image you want to copy, and then hit the Copy button in the lower right.

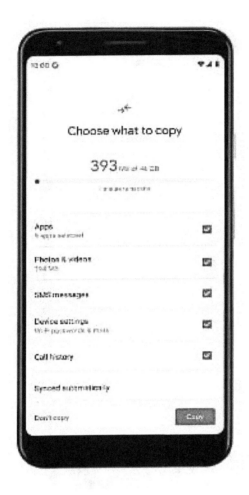

You will get an alert on your Pixel once the copy is complete.

HOW TO MAKE AND RECEIVE PHONE CALLS

The Phone app, along with other widgets and applications that display your contacts, allows you to make phone calls.

Tap the number to call it, typically, wherever you see it. If you're using Google Chrome, you may be able to copy phone numbers by tapping on highlighted ones.

Get the Phone app from the Google Play Store if you don't already have it.

- If the Phone app won't download on your smartphone, it might be because your device isn't compatible.
- Once the app is downloaded, all you have to do is follow the on-screen directions to set it as your default.

Important:

- Some languages are incompatible with talk-to-text features.
- For some of these instructions, you'll need Android 7.0 or later.

Make A Phone Call

Take Note: The phone app will not work until you accept the request to make it your default.

1. Bring up the Phone app on your mobile device.
2. Determine who should be contacted:

- A dial pad may be used to input phone numbers.
- Select a stored contact by tapping the Contacts icon. Based on your call log, we may provide you with recommended contacts to call.
- Press Recents to get a list of numbers you've phoned lately.
- Press Favourites to choose from the contacts you've stored there.

3. Press the Call button.
4. When you are done chatting, choose End call. The call bubble may be repositioned to the bottom right corner of the screen once you've minimized it.

Tip: Video calls, video conferences, and RTT calls are also possible with certain carriers and devices.

Answer Or Reject A Phone Call

- After linking your phone to Wi-Fi, you may be asked to join your carrier's network if you purchased an item from the same provider as your phone. Typically, this method takes about five minutes to get an eSIM profile.

- If your phone is locked, you may still answer calls by touching the Answer button or by sliding the white circle to the top of the screen.
- When your phone is locked, you may reject a call by swiping the white circle to the bottom of the screen or by touching Dismiss. Those whose calls go unanswered should get a message.
- You may quickly reject the call and reply with a text message by swiping up from the Message icon and selecting New message.

Tips:

- While on the phone with someone else, picking up another call puts the one you're on hold.
- You may use your voice to answer or refuse calls if you have Google Assistant turned on. Just tell Google;
- "Hey, answer the call."
- "Hey Google, reject the call."

Use Phone Call Options

With an active call:

- The dial pad will bring up the keypad.

- Pressing the Speaker button will switch between the earpiece, speakerphone, and any connected Bluetooth headphones.
- You may mute or unmute the microphone by selecting the Mute button.
- To place a call on hold without really hanging up, use the Hold button. To continue taking the call, press Hold again.

  Hint: This feature is only for those who have opted into the catch phone service. If not, a notification indicating an error will be shown on the screen.

- Press the Switch button to move between the active calls. Some are being delayed.
- Pick "Call merge" to combine all of your active calls into a single conference meeting.
- Return to the Home screen to dismiss the call.
- The call bubble may be dragged to a new location.
- The call bubble may be hidden by dragging it to the "Hide" button at the screen's bottom.
- Using certain phones and carriers, to:
- Use a video call instead: Press the video call button Call via video chat.
- Forward a ringing call to a different number:

1. Tap on Add Call when a call is in progress.
2. Type in a contact number.
3. Select Call.
4. Once the call is connected, press the Transfer button. To the number you provided in Step 2, your call is sent.

CHAPTER THREE

HOW TO MAKE PHONE CALLS WITH GOOGLE PIXEL BUDS

Use your Google Pixel Buds to make and receive calls wirelessly wherever you go. Use Clear Calling on your Pixel 7 or later smartphone to enhance the sound of the other person's voice. The call quality will be enhanced on both ends when you use the Pixel 8 or Pixel 8 Pro, which have Bluetooth Superwideband activated by default.

Answer A Phone Call

Pick up either earbud and press on it.

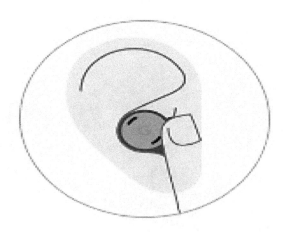

End A Phone Call

Give each earbud a double tap.

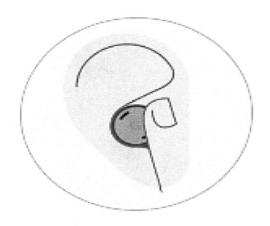

Ignore An Incoming Call

Give each earbud a double tap.

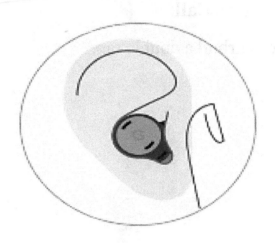

Make A Phone Call With Assistant

Needs an Android smartphone that supports Assistant.

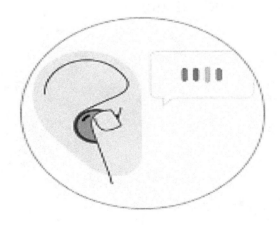

1. All you have to do to summon your Assistant is press and hold an earpiece or just say, "Hey Google."
2. Use your Contacts to instruct your Google Assistant to call a specific person. Take "Call Mom" as an example. If you haven't previously, you'll be prompted to go to your phone and activate contact permissions.

Your Assistant will start contacting the person you specified when you tell it who to call (for example, "Calling Mom") and it will confirm your request.

The Pixel Buds can't be used as a standalone headset without a second device that supports Bluetooth®. To find out what operating system and hardware are required, visit g.co/pixelbuds/help. Access to the internet is necessary. Prices can be different. Pixel Buds with the Google Assistant work only with Android devices, so you'll need an Android smartphone that supports the Assistant, a Google Account, and an active internet connection to use it. Potential data rates are applicable.

HOW TO ADD/EDIT/DELETE A CONTACT ON THE GOOGLE PIXEL 8 SERIES

1. Press the icon for the Contacts app.
2. Pick one option out of these:

- Hit the plus sign (+) to add a contact.
- To edit a contact, first find it in the list. Then, click the pencil icon.

3. Once you've finished entering or editing any of the fields (e.g., Name, Phone, Email, etc.), click Save.
   → To add a 2-second delay between numbers or wait, press *#, then choose "Pause(,)" or "Wait(;)." Finally, press the Enter icon.
   → Press on Additional fields to see more choices.

Delete A Contact

1. Press the icon for the Contacts app.
2. For each contact, choose one.
3. To delete an item, press the Menu icon.
4. To confirm, tap Move to Trash.

HOW TO TURN ON THE CLEAR CALLING FEATURE ON YOUR GOOGLE 8 SERIES

Google introduced Clear Calling as part of the Pixel Feature Drop in December 2022. We anticipate that the next Google Pixel 8 line of phones will have noise-canceling technology, which is compatible with the Pixel 7 and Pixel 7 Pro. A brief explanation of Clear Calling and instructions for configuring the function on your phone are provided here.

What Is Clear Calling?

Improved call quality for both parties is the driving force behind Google's Clear Calling feature. With the help of Google's AI, both users may enjoy the benefits of Clear Calling and noise reduction. Since the Clear Calling feature on your Pixel 8 minimizes background noise for both your speech and the other person's, not simply the noise that your microphone picks up, you can tell it's different from other features.

By eliminating ambient noise, Pixel users can make and receive calls with pristine clarity, even in busy city centers. Whether you're in a bustling city or a quiet neighborhood, it doesn't matter. Everyone can hear you crystal clear, no matter where you are.

This feature, which enhances phone conversations without being too noticeable, sets the Pixel 8 series apart from its competitors. On rare occasions, this feature may not work because the signal strength on some mobile or Wi-Fi connections is too poor.

How To Turn On Your Pixel's Clear Calling Feature

Enabling Clear Calling couldn't be easier. Turn it on, and you're good to go.

1. Launch Google's Settings app on your Pixel 8 or 8 Pro.
2. Activate the vibration and sound feature.

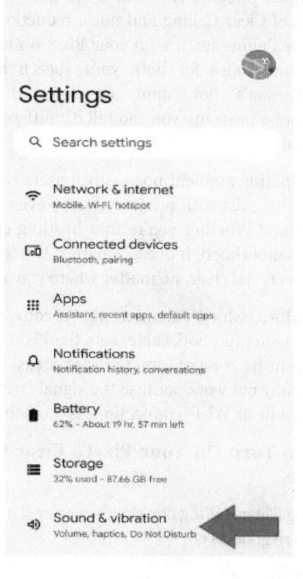

Settings

Q Search settings

📶 **Network & internet**
    Mobile, Wi-Fi, hotspot

📱 **Connected devices**
    Bluetooth, pairing

⠿ **Apps**
    Assistant, recent apps, default apps

🔔 **Notifications**
    Notification history, conversations

🔋 **Battery**
    62% - About 19 hr, 57 min left

▤ **Storage**
    32% used - 87.66 GB free

🔊 **Sound & vibration**
    Volume, haptics, Do Not Disturb

3. To end a call, scroll down and use the "Clearing" button.
4. To activate Clear Calling, just flip the toggle.

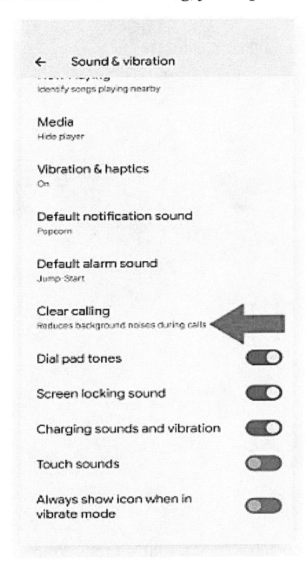

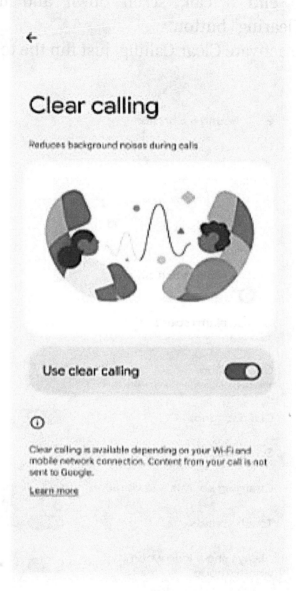

Clear calling

Reduces background noises during calls

Use clear calling

ⓘ

Clear calling is available depending on your Wi-Fi and mobile network connection. Content from your call is not sent to Google.

Learn more

There you have it; it's that simple. Your calls will now be audible.

Note: Clear Calling does not apply to all calls or in all poor scenarios since its effectiveness is dependent on your call bandwidth. The feature utilizes the audio data saved on your Google Pixel 8 or 8 Pro phone to filter out unwanted noise, although it does need enough bandwidth.

HOW TO VIEW/DELETE CALL HISTORY
1. Launch the Phone app by tapping on its icon.
2. To access the call log, tap the Recents tab.
3. Complete one or more of these tasks:
   - Eliminate Specific Calls
     1. Select the unwanted call by touching and holding it.
     2. Delete may be tapped.
     3. Use the Delete button to confirm.
   - Get Rid of Any Calls
1. To access your call history, press the Menu icon.
2. Click on the menu icon.
3. Press OK to confirm clearing your call history.

HOW TO MAKE A VIDEO CALL ON PIXEL 8 SERIES
What To Know

- There is already: To access a contact, use the Phone app. Scroll down to their name and tap the video icon.
- Choose a contact and then tap "New" to meet. To begin a video call, press the Call button.
- You may also make free video calls using Messenger, Signal, and WhatsApp.

How To Use Android's Built-In Video Calling

You may be able to make video calls straight from your phone app, but it depends on your device and provider.

1. Launch the mobile app.
2. Pick the person you want to get in touch with.
3. Click the video icon that appears next to the contact's name to initiate a video call.

4. Stay there until your contact responds. You will be instantly converted to an audio call if your contact's phone does not support video chat.

The Built-In Video Calling Capability On Android Isn't Accessible To Everyone.

Guidelines for Configuring a Google Meet Video Conference, The majority of Android phones come preinstalled with Google's video calling software, which can be accessed on Google Play. The fact that it works on both iOS and Windows means that you can have video chats with anybody. Using Meet's innovative Knock Knock feature, you can see the person you're calling even before they answer the phone. You may also use the program's built-in filters and effects.

To start a video conference with someone, just follow these steps:

1. Press on New in the app.
2. To make a call, choose a contact.
3. Press the Call button.

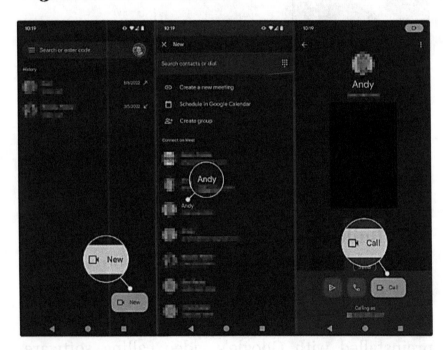

How To Video Chat On Android Using Third-Party Apps

Numerous free video-calling applications are accessible for Android users who would like not to utilize Google's offering. Facebook Messenger and WhatsApp are two excellent examples; chances are you already use one of these apps for sending or receiving messages.

The procedure of making a call using those applications, as well as others such as Signal, is quite similar. Tap the video icon when you find the person you want to speak with.

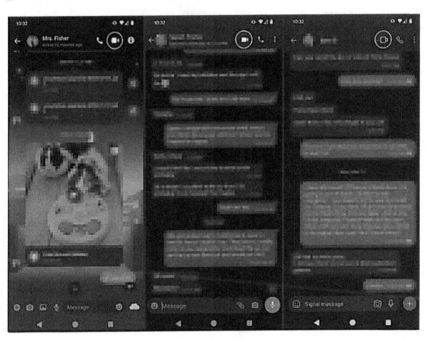

Zoom and similar video conferencing providers also have mobile chat apps that you may utilize. The main distinction is that you are required to arrange a meeting and extend invitations rather than just contacting someone. With support for up to 100 participants, Zoom is a great choice for hosting big gatherings.

Zoom for Android users, here is how to initiate a video call:

1. To start a new meeting, open the app and go to the Meetings tab.

   Note: If you aren't already logged in, go ahead and hit "Sign in" to get started.

2. Launch a Meeting by tapping the button.
3. Go to the screen's bottom and click on Participants.
4. Inviting attendees to your meeting is as easy as tapping the Invite button in the bottom left corner. A list of all your messaging applications will be shown to you. Choose the contact(s) you like to invite from this list, and Zoom will provide them with a link to attend your meeting.

Connecting to a Wi-Fi network is always preferable, regardless of the video chat software you're using. You won't go over your monthly data limit when utilizing Wi-Fi for video chats since they require a lot of bandwidth.

CHAPTER FOUR

HOW TO CONNECT TO YOUR WI-FI NETWORKS ON YOUR PIXEL PHONE

You may customize your Wi-Fi experience by adjusting the time and method your device connects.

Your device will automatically connect to neighboring Wi-Fi networks that you have previously connected to when you switch on Wi-Fi. When you're in range of a network you've stored, your smartphone may activate Wi-Fi automatically.

Note: Android 11 and later are required to complete some of these tasks.

Turn On & Connect

1. Run the Settings app on your mobile device.
2. Select Internet from the Network & Internet menu.
3. Connect to Wi-Fi.
4. Select a network from the list. The Lock icon will appear if a password is required.

- "Connected" will appear under the network name after you've connected.
- Your network has been "Saved." Your device will automatically connect to Wi-Fi when it is in range and has the feature turned on.

Tip: Another option for accessing your Wi-Fi settings is to scroll down on your device.

Establish A Connection Via Notification

With Wi-Fi enabled, alerts about nearby, reliable public networks will be sent to your device. Regarding these alerts:

- Tap Connect to establish a connection to the network.
- Select All Networks to see the Wi-Fi options menu.
- You may disable alerts for that network by clearing the notice. Get a handle on notification settings.

Hint: You have the option to connect to these networks discreetly as well. Find out how to automatically join public Wi-Fi networks.

Evaluate The Power Of Networks

Strength

1. Launch your mobile device's Settings app.
2. Go to the Network & Internet menu and choose Internet.
3. Make sure the Wi-Fi is enabled.
4. The signal strength of the network may be seen by looking for the Wi-Fi icon. A stronger signal is indicated by a stronger symbol.

Speed

1. Bring up the Settings app on your mobile device.
2. Select Internet from the Network & Internet menu.
3. Verify that the Wi-Fi is turned on.
4. The name of a public network is where you may discover the connection speed. As the signal strength changes, so may the speed.

   - You can send and receive SMS and emails, but it's slow. Views take some time to load.
   - OK: Streaming music and standard-definition (SD) movies is possible, as is reading websites and using social media.
   - Quick: You can make video calls and stream most HD videos.

- Quick: You can watch movies of excellent quality online.

Enable Nearby Saved Networks Automatically

1. Launch your mobile device's Settings app.
2. Go to the first three options: Network and Internet, Internet, and Network Preferences.
3. Enable Wi-Fi automatically. Make sure you enable Location if it isn't already. Then, enable Location services.
4. Fourth, activate Wi-Fi and Bluetooth scanning.

Tip: Wi-Fi will not activate immediately if you do:

- The site is incorrect.
- The airplane mode and battery saving are both enabled.
- "Hotspot" tethering is in the background. Wi-Fi detection is disabled.

You May Edit, Add, Share, Or Delete Registered Networks.

Update A Previously Stored Network

1. Go to the Settings app on your phone.

2. Select "Network & internet." We move on to Wi-Fi.

- Pressing on a network name will take you to that network's listing.
- Pressing on a network will bring up its settings.

Paste An Existing Network

Option 1: Hold Tight While The Network List Refreshes.

If the network you want isn't shown but is nearby, be patient and wait for the list to update.

Option 2: Integrate Network

1. Bring up the Settings app on your mobile device.
2. Select Internet from the Network & Internet menu.
3. Verify that the Wi-Fi is turned on.
4. Click "Add network" at the very bottom of the list.
5. Input the security information and network name (SSID) if prompted.
6. Press the Save button.

Help Others By Sharing Wi-Fi Details In The Settings!

1. Locate the Settings app on your smartphone.
2. Select Internet from the Network & Internet menu.
3. Before sharing, ensure that Wi-Fi is enabled and that you are linked to the network you want to use.
4. Select Settings, and then choose Share, located next to the Wi-Fi network.
5. Make sure your device can authenticate your identity if asked.
6. Use the QR code to share the Wi-Fi network.

Transfer Wi-Fi Data From The Menu

1. The Settings menu may be accessed with a swift swipe from the top of the screen.
2. Navigate to the web.
3. Turn on Wi-Fi and connect to the network you want to utilize before sharing.
4. Press and hold the Share Wi-Fi option in the bottom left corner.
5. Verify that your device can verify your identity when requested.
6. Share the Wi-Fi network with the help of the QR code.

Deleting An Existing Network

1. Go to the Settings app on your phone.

2. Select Internet from the Network & Internet menu.
3. Verify that the Wi-Fi is turned on.
4. A stored network may be touched and held.
5. Select Forget.

Join Wi-Fi Networks That Support OpenRoaming

This network of wireless hotspots is called OpenRoaming. Your Google Pixel phone may automatically connect to OpenRoaming hotspots when you're in range, providing safe, no-cost internet access to other Google users.

Configure OpenRoaming

Be advised that to configure OpenRoaming, you must be within range of an OpenRoaming network. Your phone will immediately begin connecting to any nearby OpenRoaming networks after you've finished setting it up.

Installing OpenRoaming on a Pixel phone is as follows:

1. Bring up the Settings app on your mobile device.
2. Select Internet from the Network & Internet menu.

3. Press the OpenRoaming network in the Wi-Fi list if it's within range.
4. Check the screen for any small print. 4. Hit the button labeled Continue.
5. Fifth, choose the Google account you want to use for logging in.

Disable Or Modify The OpenRoaming Configuration.

The OpenRoaming account you use might be changed, forgotten, or disconnected.

1. Get into your phone's settings when it's linked to an OpenRoaming hotspot.
2. Select Internet from the Network & Internet menu.
3. Select Settings from the menu that appears next to "OpenRoaming."
   - Select the hotspot you want to delete and then select the "Disconnect" button.
   - Choose "Forget" to disconnect from OpenRoaming permanently.
   - Go to the OpenRoaming settings menu, then tap on Advanced, and finally, Subscription, to modify your account.

Tip: Among other things, the settings page displays information about the current hotspot, such as its frequency, security, and signal strength.

How Open Roaming Works

Take note: OpenRoaming networks will not get any personally identifiable information from Google.

The OpenRoaming feature streamlines the process of connecting to public Wi-Fi hotspots. You won't need to manually accept new terms and conditions when you go between networks. The Pixel phone, on the other hand, seamlessly transitions between networks as you go from one hotspot region to another.

To become a part of OpenRoaming, networks need to agree to common terms and conditions and fulfill service and security criteria. At the time of OpenRoaming setup, you are essentially accepting these standard agreements.

Once that is done, your Pixel phone may use a Google credential to connect to OpenRoaming networks. This credential verifies that the account your phone is linked to has agreed to the rules. Your Pixel phone can now seamlessly transition between OpenRoaming hotspots thanks to this.

HOW TO PAIR YOUR PIXEL PHONE WITH YOUR DEVICE VIA BLUETOOTH.

Through the use of Bluetooth, you can wirelessly connect certain objects to your mobile device. Once a Bluetooth device has been paired once, further pairings will be automatic. If your phone is connected to anything using Bluetooth, you'll see a sign for it at the top of your screen.

Important:

- Android 10 and later are required to complete some of these procedures.
- Feel free to use your fingertips on the screen for a few of these stages.

TURN BLUETOOTH ON OR FROM THE SETTINGS APP

1. Run the Settings app on your mobile device.
2. Before you may change your connection settings, go to "Connected devices." And thereafter, Bluetooth.
3. Toggle the Bluetooth switch.

Quick Settings Is Where You Can Toggle Bluetooth On And Off.

1. Use the up arrow on the screen to swipe down.

2. The Bluetooth Quick Settings tile may be tapped or touched and held:
   - Choose the three Bluetooth devices that were most recently linked by tapping on them.
   - Rather than Disable or enable Bluetooth.
   - Feel and grasp: Launches the Settings app's "Connected devices" screen.
   a) Select Bluetooth from the list of connection choices.
   b) Rather than Disable or enable Bluetooth.

Pair A Bluetooth Accessory

The pairing process does not end until you unpair the devices.

Option 1: Make Use Of The Settings App (For All Bluetooth Devices)

1. Run the Settings app on your mobile device.
2. After selecting "Connected devices," go to "Connection preferences," and finally, turn Bluetooth on. To begin, toggle Bluetooth on. Your device may be located by adjacent devices when you enable Bluetooth in your device's settings.
3. Press on the "Pair new device" button.

4. To connect a Bluetooth device to your mobile device, tap on its name.
5. Proceed as directed on the screen.

Tip: Try the most frequent passcodes, "0000" or "1234", if you require a passcode but don't have it.

Option 2: Make Use Of Alerts (Fast Pair Accessories Only)

1. Make sure
   - Verify that your Bluetooth item is compatible with Fast Pair mode. Fast Pair-compatible accessories will clearly state this on the packaging. A lot of them also state "Made for Google" or "Made by Google."
   - The Android version on your mobile device is 6.0 or later.
   - You have enabled Bluetooth and Location on your mobile device.
2. Get your Fast Pair device into pairing mode and power it on. Hold your device (phone or tablet) close to your attachment.
3. Select "Tap to pair" from the notification menu.
4. A notice stating "Device connected" or "Pairing complete" will be sent to you.

5. Tap Set up now if you need to set up your attachment.

Hint: Locate the "Connected devices" section of your phone's settings menu if you aren't receiving any alerts. To connect a gadget, find it under "Nearby devices" and touch it.

Option 2: Connect

1. Run the Settings app on your mobile device.
2. After selecting "Connected devices," go to "Connection preferences," and finally, turn Bluetooth on.
3. To begin, toggle Bluetooth on.
4. Select a paired but disconnected device from the list of devices.
5. Once your devices are linked, you'll see the status "Connected."

RENAME, LINK, OR DEACTIVATE A BLUETOOTH DEVICE

Select Actions, Rename, Or Unpair A Bluetooth Item.

1. Launch your mobile device's Settings app.
2. After choosing "Connected devices," go to "Connection preferences," and lastly, enable Bluetooth.

3. Go into your Bluetooth device's settings:

•Scroll down to the "Saved Devices" area to locate your attachment. After that, find your device and hit the Settings button that comes up next to it.

If "Saved devices" does not include any accessories, press See all. Select the gear icon () that appears next to the item's name.

4. Make any changes you desire:

To change the accessory's name, go to Edit > Edit settings > pencil in the menu at the top.

Click "Disconnect" to cut off the connection.

To remove the app from your phone or tablet for good, just hit the "Forget" button.

On some devices, you may have the ability to turn additional settings on or off.

Modify The Bluetooth Name Of Your Mobile Device.

1. Run the Settings app on your mobile device.
2. After selecting "Connected devices," go to "Connection preferences," and finally, turn Bluetooth on.
3. To begin, toggle Bluetooth on.

4. Press the name of the machine.

5. Change the name.

6. Select the option to rename.

HOW TO SHARE A MOBILE CONNECTION BY TETHERING OR A HOTSPOT ON PIXEL

Connecting several devices to the internet is as easy as using your phone's mobile data. Tethering, or making use of a hotspot, is another name for this method of sharing a connection.

- The Settings app on most Android phones allows you to share mobile data over Wi-Fi, Bluetooth, or USB.
- By using notifications, all Pixel and select Nexus phones can share mobile data over Wi-Fi.
- The ability to tether a Wi-Fi connection to multiple devices is also available on Pixel 3 and subsequent Pixel phones.

Caution: Tethering may be subject to additional charges or limitations imposed by some cell carriers. Get in touch with your carrier for further information.

Important: You'll need Android 9.0 or later to complete any of these tasks.

HOW TO TETHER BY WI-FI HOTSPOT
Reach For The Settings App.

Step 1: Get The Mobile Hotspot Feature Going.

Important: Please off Data Saver if you have already done so to tether over Wi-Fi.

1. Bring up the Settings app on your mobile device.
2. Navigate to Hotspot & tethering, then Wi-Fi hotspot, under Network & internet.
3. Saddle up the Wi-Fi hotspot.
4. By tapping on it, you may access or modify the hotspot's settings, such as its name or password.

Tip: If you'd want your hotspot to not need a password, you may do so by selecting None under "Security."

Step 2: Join More Devices To Your Phone's Wireless Network.

1. Launch the Wi-Fi settings menu on the other device.
2. Determine the name of your phone's hotspot.
3. Put in the passcode for your mobile hotspot.
4. To connect, click the icon.

Hint: Your phone's mobile data may be shared with up to ten additional devices when you use it as a Wi-Fi hotspot.

Use Notifications

Step 1: Verify That Your Devices Are Capable Of Tethering Via Notification Systems.

Verify that alerts may be received by your phone about shared mobile data. Here are the phones that qualify:

- Pixel smartphones
- Tablet Google Pixel C
- Various Nexus models, including 5X, 6P, 6, and 9

Step 2: Use Alerts To Set Up Tethering.

Step 1: Use The Same Account Across All Gadgets.

1. Remember to sign in with your Google Account on all of your devices.
2. Bluetooth and Wi-Fi must be enabled. Find out how to activate them.

Step 2: Open Up Your Phone's Network To Other Devices.

1. Bring up the Settings app on your mobile device.
2. To get instant tethering, tap on Google.
3. Activate the data connection provider.

Step 3: Open Up Your Phone's Connection To All Of Your Other Devices.

1. Launch the Settings app on the other smartphone.
2. To get instant tethering, tap on Google.
3. To activate the "Get data connection" feature, turn it on.

Advice: Most devices that support this kind of tethering have it enabled by default.

Step 3: Use Alerts To Tether.

Step 1: Get All Of Your Gadgets Ready.

- Ensure that all devices are configured to tether via alerts (as mentioned above).
- Always have your mobile data-enabled phone on hand.
- Get the device you want to link unlocked.

Step 2: On The Competing Device That Isn't Linked

- A notice reading "Wi-Fi hotspot available" appears on your screen. Press on it and then proceed as directed.
- Access Google And from the Settings app, then choose Instant Tethering to connect later without the alert. In the subsequent step, your mobile device Following that, Get in touch.
- When prompted, choose Continue to proceed with carrier verification.

Step 3: When Using Mobile Data On Your Phone

- A "Sharing data connection" alert will appear as soon as you establish the connection. So long as you maintain a connection, this message will remain.
- When prompted, hit the "Disconnect" button to end the connection.

Hint: An Instant Tethering connection will automatically terminate after about 10 minutes of inactivity. Get the lowdown on troubleshooting Wi-Fi hotspots.

HOW TO TETHER BY BLUETOOTH

1. Connect your mobile device to the other.

2. Get the second device ready to use Bluetooth to connect to the network. Read and follow the device's manual carefully.
3. Bring up the Settings app on your mobile device.
4. Select "Network & internet." Finally, we have hotspots and tethering.
5. Hover over Bluetooth tethering.

Connect With A USB Cord

Take Note: USB tethering with Android is not compatible with Mac machines.

1. Link your mobile phone to the alternate gadget using a USB cord. The top of the screen displays a notice that reads "Connected as a...".
2. Bring up the Settings app on your mobile device.
3. Select "Network & internet." Finally, we have hotspots and tethering.
4. Please enable USB tethering.

Turn Off Your Hotspot Without Touching A Button

Important: When no devices are connected, your hotspot switches off to preserve battery life.

1. Bring up the Settings app on your mobile device.
2. Navigate to Hotspot & tethering, then Wi-Fi hotspot, under Network & internet.
3. Press the "Turn off hotspot automatically" button to enable or disable this feature.

Tip: Keep your gadgets plugged in when tethering and disconnect them after you're through.

CHAPTER FIVE

HOW TO ENABLE/DISABLE/MODIFY SCREEN LOCK ON PIXEL 8 SERIES

1. Launch the app called Settings.
2. Security & privacy ~Device unlock~ Screen lock.
    → If prompted to add a Google™ account, do one of the following:
    - To create an account, tap the "Add Google account now" button.
    - Tap You may continue without creating an account if you choose.
    → Punch in the current pattern, PIN, or security code if prompted.
3. Pick one of these options:
    - Pattern Setup
       1. Pattern of Taps.
       2. Select Next once you've drawn an unlock pattern that joins a minimum of four dots.
       3. Redraw the pattern in the same way and hit the Confirm button.

4. When asked, choose a notification choice and then hit OK.

- Configure PIN
  1. Press the PIN key.
  2. Select Next after entering a 4- to 16-digit numeric PIN.
  3. To confirm, enter the numeric PIN again.
  4. When asked, choose a notification choice and then hit OK.

- Create a Password
  1. Select Password.
  2. Choose a password between 4 and 16 characters long, and then hit the Next button.
  3. Press Confirm after re-entering the password.
  4. When asked, choose a notification choice and then hit OK.

- Remove the Caption Lock
  1. Select 'None' or 'Swipe'.
  2. Then, choose "Yes, remove" to confirm.

HOW TO CUSTOMIZE YOUR PIXEL 8 SERIES HOME SCREEN

Install Programs

Note: The only way to add a widget to your Home screen is to create a shortcut to a specific contact or bookmark.

1. Swipe up from the center of the Home screen to see all applications.
2. Grab an app using your finger.
3. Move the shortcut to your chosen Home screen by dragging and dropping it.
   → Please ensure that the chosen Home screen has enough room to accommodate the app before proceeding with the addition. You may add more Home screen panels if you need to.

Import Widgets

Note: You may add mini-apps called widgets to your home screen. Some examples of widgets include weather, clock, calendar, and others. Since they often show information and occupy more real estate than a single icon, they differ from shortcuts.

1. Press and hold an empty area on the Home screen.
2. Select Widgets.
3. Choose a group, and then tap and hold a widget to make it yours.

4. Release the widget after dragging it to the Home screen of your choice.

→ The widget can't be added unless there's enough room on the screen. You may add more home screen panels if you need to.

5. To activate the widget, touch on any further choices that may be available.

→ The kind of widget determines the available options.

Move Or Insert Folders

1. Press and hold an app (such as Email, My Verizon, etc.) on the Home screen.

2. Release the app after dragging it to another program (like Gmail or Call Filter, for example).

→ An unnamed folder is created to store the shortcuts. Renaming the folder:

a. Click on the folder.

b. At the very bottom of the open folder, you should see the Title bar. Tap on it.

c. Click the Done button (bottom right) once you've entered a name.

→ You may delete an entire folder by dragging its contents out of another folder.

Get Rid Of Widgets And Apps

1. Select the widget, program, or other object from the Home screen by touching and holding it.
2. Move the item to the "Remove" tab (located at the top) and then let go.

Set Wallpaper

1. Press and hold an empty area on the Home screen.
2. Press on Wallpaper and style.
   → Select ALLOW when asked for permission.
3. After tapping More wallpapers, choose the folder (My photographs, Landscapes, etc.) that contains the wallpapers you want to use.
4. Choose a picture.
5. The Preview screen will include tabs that you may use to examine:
   • Starting screen
   • Secure screen
6. Pick a wallpaper style from the options shown after tapping the Set Wallpaper button (top right):
   • Starting screen
   • Secure screen
   • Screens for home and security

HOW TO SET LOCK SCREEN NOTIFICATIONS ON GOOGLE PIXEL 8 SERIES

1. Launch the app from the Store.
2. Choose "Notifications"
3. From the lock screen, tap Notifications, and then choose an option:

→ Different types of screen locks may provide different options.

- Default, show chats, and silence
- Conceal your private chats and alerts
- Do not display any alerts

HOW TO SET UP FINGERPRINT ON YOUR PIXEL 8 SERIES

Step 1

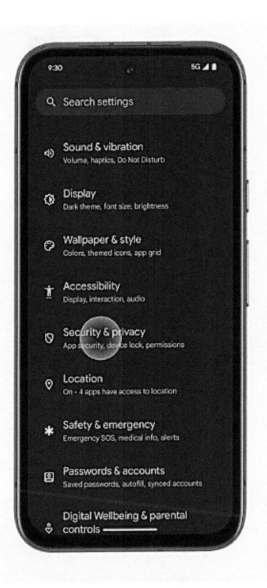

To enable fingerprint authentication on your Pixel, launch the Settings app and go to Security & privacy.

Step 2

Tap the device to unlock it.

Step 3

Unlock using a Fingerprint or Face.

Step 4

An additional PIN, pattern, or password will be requested if you haven't previously configured a screen lock.

Choose "Fingerprint Unlock" from the menu.

Step 5

Please study the operation of Fingerprint Unlock. After you're done, find the "I agree" button and touch it.

Step 6

You will be asked to configure your fingerprint on the screen that follows. Press the Start button.

Step 7

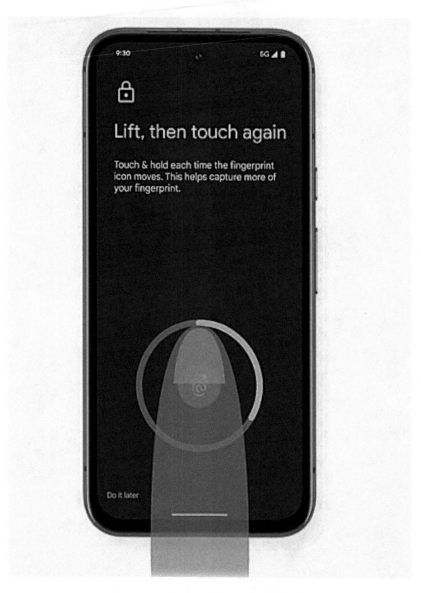

To activate the sensor, press and hold it until it lights up and your smartphone vibrates.

Tip: A thick screen protector or very intense outside light can be the blame if your fingerprint scanner isn't working properly.

Step 8

At each change in the fingerprint symbol, raise your finger and press and hold it on the sensor. Place the sides of your finger on the sensor as instructed, then gently shift your finger position each time.

Tip: moisturize your fingertips before scanning if they are really dry.

Step 9

Press "Done" once you've inserted your fingerprint.

If you want to utilize a different hand or finger for unlocking, you may add other fingerprints.

HOW TO SET UP FACE RECOGNITION ON PIXEL 8 SERIES

- To open the gadget, facial recognition is used.
- Make sure you're inside or out of the direct sunshine for the best results.
- This feature may or may not be available depending on your IT administrator's rules when syncing to a company Exchange account.
- Before you proceed with the procedures below, make sure a secure lock type has been set up. Facial unlock is disabled when the security lock is turned off.

1. Swipe up from the Home screen to see all the applications.
2. Move around on the Options Menu iconProtection and confidentialityFree your device.
3. Select Unlock with Face and Fingerprint.
4. Put in your current pattern, PIN, or password.
5. Select Face Unlock.
6. Complete one of these tasks:
    - For initial configuration:
        1. Find the information you need, and then hit the "I agree" button.
        → You may have to scroll a little.

2. Once you've reviewed the information, hit the Start button.

3. To participate, read the disclaimer and then tap I agree/Confirm or Skip on the "Help made Face Unlock better" box.

4. Position your face inside the on-screen circle while holding the phone 8-20 inches away.

5. Tap Done from the 'Looks nice!' box.

- To remove face data

    1. Tap the Delete face model from the 'Face Unlock' option to delete face data.

    2. Please read the disclaimer and then hit the Delete button to confirm.

HOW TO SET SCREEN LOCK ON YOUR PIXEL SERIES 8

An additional layer of protection for your Android device is the ability to configure a screen lock. A PIN, pattern, or password will often be requested whenever you power on your device or activate the screen. You may be able to use your face or fingerprint to unlock some gadgets.

Important:

- Android 10 and later are required to complete some of these procedures.

- Feel free to use your fingertips on the screen for a few of these stages.

Set Or Change A Screen Lock

Important: Using a PIN, pattern, or password with your screen lock will encrypt your automatic and manual backups, so be careful to do this.

1. Go to your device's settings.
2. Press the Setting and Security button.
3. Press the Screen lock to choose a screen lock type.
   - Selecting a new lock requires entering your PIN, pattern, or password if you have already established one.
4. To lock the screen, just tap on the lock icon. Proceed as directed by the on-screen prompts.
5. Next to "Screen lock," tap Settings to see your screen lock's configuration. A lock screen message, automated lock time, and the ability to lock the power button are all configurable.

Screen Lock Options

No Lock

- This option does not lock your phone. It doesn't protect you, but it gets you to the home screen fast.

- Use your finger to drag the screen from side to side. It doesn't protect you, but it gets you to the home screen fast.

Standard Locks

1. PIN: Type in four or more digits; however, for extra protection, a six-digit PIN is suggested. Generally speaking, longer PINs are safer.
2. Design: Use your finger to make a basic design.
3. Password: Please input a combination of at least four characters, including spaces. For maximum protection, use a strong password whenever you lock your screen.

CHAPTER SIX

HOW TO USE THE PIXEL 8 COMMON CAMERA SETTINGS

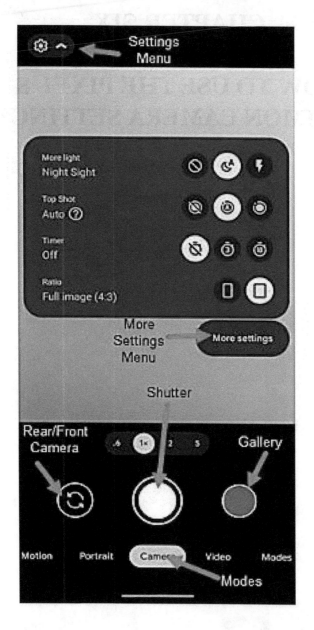

Settings

- To access the camera, go to the Home screen and touch the symbol in the bottom right corner.
  - → If it isn't already there, swipe vertically from the middle of the screen and then press Camera.
- Press the symbol that appears as a drop-down menu in the Settings app.
- Choose an option and tweak it to your liking, or use the toggles to toggle between on and off:
1. More light
2. Top Shot
3. Timer
4. Ratio
5. More settings
   - Save location
   - Camera sounds
   - Google Lens suggestions
   - Social Share
   - Gestures
   - Frequent Faces
   - Device storage
   - Advanced
   - Framing hints
   - Grid type

- White balance
- Exposure
- Camera photo resolution
- Save the selfie as previewed
- Videos stabilization

Motion

- To access the camera, go to the Home screen and touch the symbol in the bottom right corner.
1. If it isn't already there, swipe vertically from the middle of the screen and then press Camera.
   - Press the symbol that appears as a drop-down menu in the Settings app.
   - Press the Motion symbol that best fits your needs.

- Motion off
- Motion auto
- Motion on

Timer

1. To access the camera, go to the Home screen and touch the symbol in the bottom right corner.
   → If it isn't already there, swipe vertically from the middle of the screen and then press Camera.
2. Press the symbol that appears as a drop-down menu in the Settings app.
3. Select a timer by tapping on its icon:

- off
- 3 sec
- 10 sec

Flash

1. To access the camera, go to the Home screen and touch the symbol in the bottom right corner.
   → If it isn't already there, swipe vertically from the middle of the screen and then press Camera.

2. Press the symbol that appears as a drop-down menu in the Settings app.
3. Press on a Flash symbol like the ones below:

- None
- Night Sight
- Flash on

Switch Camera

1. Select the Camera icon from the Home screen.
   → In that case, scroll up to see all applications, and then hit Camera.
2. Select the symbol that looks like a camera facing left or right. Camera Facing allows you to toggle between the front- and back-facing cameras.

Shooting Modes

1. Select the Camera icon from the Home screen.
   → In that case, scroll up to see all applications, and then hit Camera.

2. Swipe to the left or right to choose a different camera mode:
   - Night Sight
   - Long Exposure
   - Portrait
   - Camera
   - Video
   - Select a mode by tapping on the corresponding option:
     o Lens
     o Panorama
     o Photosphere

HOW TO USE YOURPIXEL PHONE AS A WEBCAM

If you have a data-compatible USB cord, you can turn your Pixel phone into a camera. When your phone is in webcam mode, it functions similarly to a standard webcam. The camera is compatible with all devices that have the USB Video Class (UVC) feature, including computers, televisions, vehicles, and other mobile devices.

Convert Your Mobile Device Into A Webcam

1. Hook up your mobile phone to your electronic gadget using a USB cord that supports data transfer.

2. When prompted, choose the option to "Charge this device through USB" on your mobile device.

3. Choose "Webcam" from the "Use USB for" menu.

Advice: Hit the Webcam notice in the upper right of your screen to preview and tweak your webcam.

Explore The Many Ways Your Pixel Phone May Serve As A Webcam.

- Even when in webcam mode, you may use your phone as usual. Toggle between applications or disable the screen altogether.
- The webcam feed will halt if you have a video call or are using an app that needs a camera. You will see a camera access prohibited logo on the webcam broadcast, but it will instantly restart when you finish.
- While in webcam mode, your phone charges normally using USB.
- The ability to utilize your phone's camera as a webcam with other Pixel devices is not yet available. Pixel smartphones do not support UVC cameras.

HOW TO UTILIZE LIVE TRANSCRIPTION

On an Android smartphone, you have the option to utilize Live Transcribe, which allows you to record audio and display it as text.

Launch Live Transcribe After Downloading.

Important: Be sure to jump down to the Pixel section if you're using a Pixel phone.

1. Get Live Transcribe & Sound Notifications from the Google Play Store on your device.
2. Locate the Apps tab.
3. Press the Live Transcribe icon. Instant Transcript.
4. Verify that you have an active internet connection.
5. Place the microphone on your device close to the subject or source of sound you want to record. The microphone is most often found on the underside of your electronic gadget.

Pixel: Make Live Transcription Active

Pixel phones and several other Android phones come with Live Transcribe preinstalled. Activate Live Transcribe by following these instructions:

1. Launch the Settings app on your smartphone.

2. Press on Accessibility, and then on Live Transcribe.
3. Press the Open Live Transcribe button.
4. Tap OK to confirm the permissions.
5. Altering your shortcut in Live Transcribe is an optional feature. Discover the ins and outs of accessible shortcuts.
6. A two-finger swipe up or a push on the Accessibility button will bring up your Live Transcribe shortcut.
7. Verify that you have an active internet connection.
8. Place the microphone on your device close to the subject or source of sound you want to record. The microphone is most often found on the underside of your electronic gadget.

HOW TO USE LIVE TRANSCRIBE OFFLINE
Get Languages To Use While You're Not Online.

When you're somewhere with spotty internet service, like on a trip, it's a good idea to download several languages to use offline. Aside from that, it preserves your mobile data plan.

Important:

- You may download numerous languages, including English, French, and more, for offline usage on some Android smartphones and all Pixel devices running Android 12 or later.
- You may download English for offline usage on some Android smartphones running Android 8, 9, 10, or 11.

1. Launch Live Transcribe on your mobile device.
2. Select More Settings from the list of options, then touch Settings at the bottom.
3. Press on "Primary language" and then "Secondary language."

- **Here is the link to download:**
  o This symbol indicates that the language is accessible for download if it occurs at the end of the list.
  o A language is not accessible for download if it does not include this symbol at the end.
- What this means is that you are downloading the language.
- "Done" indicates that the language file has been successfully downloaded.

Set Offline Mode Preference

With Live Transcribe, offline transcription is immediately enabled to provide a seamless transcribing experience. Just follow these procedures if you want to make it online.

1. Get Live Transcribe up and running on your tech. Instant Transcript.
2. Select More Settings from the list of options, then touch Settings at the bottom.
3. Select Offline transcriptions from the Advanced menu at the bottom.
4. Activate Transcribe online.

Advice:

- You may utilize the downloaded languages in offline mode at all times, regardless of whether you have an internet connection or not, as long as you enable Transcribe offline.
- Live Transcribe will intelligently toggle between online and offline modes for the languages you've downloaded when you disable Transcribe offline. This behavior is dependent on the stability of your network.

Keep Track Of Your Transcribing Work

Note: After 24 hours, your transcriptions will be destroyed if you turn off transcription history. Live

Transcribe does not allow you to export transcriptions. Text may be copied and pasted, however.

For three days, Live Transcribe keeps a record of your transcriptions. It will be automatically removed after three days, and you have the option to remove your transcription history at any moment. Just scroll up to see all of your transcriptions.

You may be certain that the audio and transcriptions recorded in the Live Transcribe app are secured and kept safe.

CHAPTER SEVEN

HOW TO TRANSLATE SPEECH AND TEXT ON YOUR PIXEL 8 SERIES

If you own a Pixel 6 or later, including Fold, you can translate live video and text chats.

Make Live Translate Active.

1. Run the Settings app on your mobile device.
2. Select System, followed by Live Translate.
3. Activate the Live Translate feature. Turning on Live Translate is the default setting.
4. Extra not included: Change the default target language to another one:
   a. Click on Translate to.
   b. Choose a tongue.
   c. Press the language option.
5. Extra not included: Provide more languages for source code to work with:
   a. Press the "Add a language" button.
   b. Choose a tongue.
   c. Press the language option.

List Of Languages That Live Translate Supports

- Chat: AR, DA, DE, EN, ES, FA, FR, HI, IT, JP, KO, NL, PL, PT, RU, SV, TH, TR, VI, zh_CN, and zh-TW
- Media: DE, EN, ES, FR, IT, and JP
- Interpreter Mode: DE, EN, ES, FR, IT, and JP

Translate Text Messages

You may translate text messages on some chat applications by turning on Live Translate. Every translation is done locally on the device.

Simply tapping the language bubble will toggle between the original and your selected language.

To modify available languages:

1. Get started with a multilingual text chat.
2. To translate, press the translation chip.
3. Please revise the languages used for translation in the drop-down menu.

Just one message needs to be translated:

1. Launch a multilingual text message.
2. Choose text by touching and holding.
3. Just press the copy button.
4. Select Translate from the menu.

Hint: you may translate the whole page by tapping the drop-down menu and selecting Translate Complete page.

Use Your Camera As A Translator

Using your camera, you may interpret language seen on menus and signage.

1. Just press Lens on your Pixel's search bar. The Google Lens.
2. Simply snap a picture of the words you want to translate.

Caption Translation For Various Media

By tapping the live caption, you may change the caption language for media such as podcasts, video calls, voice messages, and videos. Simply press and hold the volume button until you see the Live Caption option. Subtitles with live captioning.

Use Your Pixel Fold's Interpreter Mode To See Real-Time Translations.

Turn on interpreter mode with Google Assistant on your Pixel phone and share your translation with someone else.

Important: Avoid covering the microphone if you want accurate translations when using a split screen.

To use Google Assistant for translation:

1. Bring out your phone.
2. Just say "Hey Google" followed by a command, such as :
   - "Please translate this into Italian for me."
   - "What does 'house' mean in Spanish?"
   - "Activate the modus operandi." Find the language you want translated.
3. To access the microphone, go to the bottom of the screen and touch the Dual screen.
4. Keep to your native tongue. An external screen will display a translation of your spoken words to the other party.

For the external screen translations to cease, you have the option to:

- Press the button for two screens once more.
- Apps that are switched
- Turn off all applications
- Put down your phone

HOW TO TRANSLATE TEXT TO SPEECH WITH LIVE CAPTION
Saddle Up With Real-Time Captioning

To use Live Caption, you need:

- Google Pixel 2 and subsequent Android smartphones with an English user interface
- Versions of the Pixel 6 and Pixel 6 Pro smartphones are available in Japanese, Spanish, French, German, Italian, and English
  - You may also use the auto-detection feature on the Pixel 6 and Pixel 6 Pro to recognize certain languages and have media captions translated automatically.
- Other specific Android devices To enable or disable Live Caption:

Lift the device's headphone jack.

1. Press the Live Caption Live
2. The caption Subtitles button is located under the volumes.

Hint: Make sure to enable Live Caption in your device's Accessibility settings if these procedures do not resolve the issue.

With Live Caption enabled, any audio in media playing on your device will have subtitles superimposed over it.

During calls, subtitles also show up on Pixel phones. An announcement is made to the other party on the call to let them know that captions are enabled.

Your device never stores or transmits any captions; they are handled locally.

Advice: Check to see whether Android System Intelligence has been updated if "Live Caption" is still not visible. Known formerly as "Device Personalization Services," Android System Intelligence has now changed its name. The app may still be updated even if the Play Store still shows the prior name.

Shift The Caption Container

- Hold down the screen button and drag it up or down to reposition the caption box.
- You may disable Live Caption and conceal captions by dragging the caption box from the screen's bottom.
- Use the double-tap gesture to enlarge or minimize the caption box. While you're on the phone, you can't use this motion.

Change Live Caption Settings

1. Launch Settings on your mobile device.
2. Proceed to Live Caption by tapping on Sound.
3. The following options are accessible via the Settings menu:
   - Adjust the level of live captioning.
   - Keep vulgarity to a minimum.
   - Sound labels, like those for applause and laughing, may be shown or hidden.
   - Adjust the volume while hiding or showing the Live Caption symbol.
   - Enable or disable call captioning. Only Pixel phones have this option.

Hint: Head over to caption settings to tweak the size, style, and color of the captions.

Respond To A Phone Call By Typing

Note: This feature is only compatible with the Pixel 6, Pixel 6 Pro, Pixel 6a, and Pixel Fold.

Make calls silently by using this function. With real-time captioning, you may put in answers to the other person's words. The system reads out your messages. You are limited to speaking in your current language since this function does not translate.

1. Go into your phone's Settings to enable typing replies.
2. Select Live Caption from the Accessibility menu.
3. For calls, enable type replies.

When call captions are enabled, you will get a notice. Press the Keyboard Keyboard to begin typing.

Battery Life And Further Remarks

Live Caption drains battery life while you're on a call or playing media. When you're in power conservation mode, Live Caption will immediately disable.

Other information about Live Caption:

- You should only use Live Caption on calls with a single other person.
- The captions disclosure notification will be muffled if you mute your side of the call while it is being made. Verify that the other individual is aware that the captions are enabled.
- Unfortunately, not all media and calling applications support captions.

- Clear voice and little background noise are ideal for Live Caption to function.
- Music is not compatible with Live Caption.
- No data plan or internet connection is required for Live Caption. No data is ever sent or saved to Google; all processing of audio and captions occurs on the device itself.

CHAPTER EIGHT

HOW TO USE THE GOOGLE PIXEL 8 CAMERA

With a Pixel phone or tablet, you have access to a plethora of sophisticated picture editing tools.

Use Framing Cues To Snap A Perfectly Vertical Shot.

When the two lines intersect at a zero angle, your phone will be in a perfectly horizontal position for taking pictures.

1. Kick off your Google Camera app.
2. Always keep your phone steady. In the center of the screen, two lines—one yellow and one white—appear.
3. Simply tilting your phone forward or backward and rotating it from left to right will bring the lines together.
4. The "Up/Down" indication will show up if you tilt your phone horizontally or vertically toward your topic.
5. Turn your phone from left to right and tilt it forward and backward to line up the

"Up/Down" indication and capture a straight shot.

You May Toggle The Leveling Of The Horizon And The Up/Down Indication On And Off.

1. Kick off your Google Camera app.
2. Press Settings in the lower left corner.
3. To access further options, tap on that option.
4. Make framing suggestions invisible.

Pro Controls Allow You To Alter The Appearance Of Your Images.

The slider located at the bottom of each picture allows you to modify the photos:

- Aperture
- Focus
- ISO

Get A Picture With A Lot Of Detail (50 MP)

You have complete control over the exposure, color, and other features of your photographs, and they may be captured at a high quality of 50 MP.

To enable high-definition:

1. Kick off your Google Camera app.

2. Tap on Settings in the bottom left, and then choose the Pro option.

3. Prioritize a Resolution of 50 MP.

Use The Portrait Mode To Snap A Picture Of Yourself.

To capture portraits:

1. Kick off your Google Camera app.

2. Press Portrait, and then Capture, in the picture mode carousel.

To make the backdrop of your shot less noticeable:

1. Launch the Google Photos mobile app.

2. Select Images.

3. Go to Tools > Blur in the Edit menu.

4. Slide the Blur slider to adjust the blurring effect.

Advice: The front-facing camera on a Pixel Tablet is the only one that supports Portrait mode.

Retouch Your Face Photographs To Make Them Seem Better.

Change the texture of your skin, the tone beneath your eyes, and the brightness of your eyes with the help of Face Retouching.

Click the "Face Retouching" button:

1. Kick off your Google Camera app.
2. To access the face retouching options, go to the Portrait menu, then hit Settings.
3. Pick a choice:
   - Off
   - Soft
   - Sleek

HOW TO ADJUST YOUR CAMERA LENS
Use The Ultrawide Zoom To Get A Broader View.

Take Note: You can only use this function on Pixel 4a (5G) and newer models.

Ultrawide Zoom allows you to capture a wider range of subjects and environments.

1. Kick off your Google Camera app.
2. You may zoom out on your screen by pinching it.

Vary The Subject's Sharpness With The Auto-Focus Feature.

1. Simply pointing the camera at the topic will bring it into sharp focus.

2. Press the topic. In tandem with the topic, a white circle emerges and glides across the screen.
3. To fixate on a moving subject and lock exposure and focus, use the Lock button.

Tip: If you're using an accessibility feature, you may double-tap the screen to bring the focus and exposure of your shot to the subject.

Shoot A Wide Shot

1. Kick off your Google Camera app.
2. Locate the Panorama option on the picture mode carousel.
3. Select Record.
4. Maintain a solid grip on the lens while you horizontally shift the camera. Maintain proper alignment of the white frame.
   - Turn your phone vertically to capture a panoramic shot from above. Next, tilt your camera vertically.
5. Hit Stop recording after you're through taking the picture.

Hint: Press Close Close to delete a picture.

Go All The Way Around With A Picture Sphere

Be Advised: that this function is only compatible with Pixel 3 through Pixel 7a.

You can make panoramic picture spheres, fisheye photographs, and other varieties of 360-degree photo spheres with your Pixel camera. How to make a picture sphere that can be rotated 360 degrees:

1. Kick off your Google Camera app.
2. Select Photo Sphere from the photo mode carousel, and then press Capture.
3. Place the target circle on top of a white dot. After the dot becomes blue, it will vanish.
4. Holding the lens steady, advance the camera to the next white dot.
5. Keep going until you see no more white dots, or press the "Done" button.

For a different kind of Photo Sphere:

- Go to the very bottom left and hit the Settings button.
- If you want a picture that shows every angle, you may use the Panorama photo sphere feature.
- Select Horizontal to snap a wide-angle shot.
- Select "Vertical" to snap a shoot in portrait mode.

- To capture a shot with a broad perspective, choose Wide-angle.
- Tap Fisheye to capture a shot with a fisheye effect.

Get Up Close And Personal With Macro Focus

Be Advised: that this function is exclusive to Pixel 7 Pro and subsequent models.

When shooting images or videos, use Macro Focus to get those little details, like dew droplets or flower petals.

For Macro Focus to work:

1. Kick off your Google Camera app.
2. Keep your gadget near the object you're trying to capture.
3. To center the screen, tap it.
4. Snap a picture or record a movie as soon as the Macro flower blooms.

Tips:

- Be careful not to obstruct the light or shadow your subject.
- Press to activate or deactivate Macro Focus.

- You may pinch to zoom in on a certain area of your topic by tapping the screen.
- Auto Night Sight is compatible with this function as well.

Record Footage Or Stills From A Distance

Take pictures of things when you're far away. A few Pixel smartphones include the next-gen zoom lens technology, which allows you to zoom up to 30x.

Tips: If you zoom in on your Pixel 7 Pro, Pixel 8 Pro, or Pixel Fold phone to 15x, you'll see that zoom stabilization activates automatically.

1. Turn on your camera. Google Photo.
2. Focus on your topic.
   - For easy modifications: Press the 2x or 5x zoom button located above the shutter button.
   - To get a better idea: You may reveal the zoom slider by pinching the screen or swiping over the buttons.
3. Focus by tapping on your object.
4. Snap a picture.

Hint: Use bright light for the best results when using zoom and stabilization on your camera.

HOW TO EDIT A PHOTO OR VIDEO ON YOUR PIXEL 8 SERIES

If you have a Pixel smartphone, you can alter the appearance of photos. In your Google Photos library, you can also find and modify images shot with other devices, as well as those that are more recent.

Alter The Picture Format To Either RAW Or JPEG.

When you turn on the RAW/JPEG option in your camera's settings, it will store your images in both the JPEG and RAW formats. You can easily distinguish between your RAW and JPEG photographs by looking for the RAW symbol at the top of your photo library.

To make RAW and JPEG files usable:

1. Launch the Google Camera app.
2. Press Settings, followed by More Settings, in the bottom left corner.
3. Scroll down to "General options," and then choose Advanced.
4. Save the image as a raw or jpeg.

Hint: The Pixel 8 Pro doesn't need this step.

To enable RAW:

1. If you're in picture mode, go to the bottom left and touch on Settings.
2. Disable JPEG only and enable RAW.

To access, see, and make changes to a RAW file:

1. Launch the Google Photos mobile app.
2. When you see a "RAW" flag in the gallery grid, it means that the photos in the RAW + JPEG sets were captured with the RAW option enabled.
3. Select "View" to see RAW.
   - The JPEG picture is shown, but if you want to see the RAW image, you may do so by tapping on the second tile.
4. Press modify to modify RAW.
   - From inside Google Photos, you may establish a Default RAW Editor for use with your preferred editor when working with RAW files.

Tip: Remember that your RAW photographs will be automatically backed up in Google Photos if you activate backup.

To work with RAW files:

1. Grab a shot using either the basic or Night Sight modes.

2. Back to your home screen, you go.
   - Navigating via gestures: Pull up the screen by swiping up from the bottom.
   - Using three or two buttons for navigation: Press the Home button.
3. Launch Google Images.
4. Press on Library, and then on Raw, in the lower right corner.

Fix, Crop, Or Straighten An Image.

To Fix Crooked Shots, Use Gridlines.

1. Launch the Google Camera app.
2. Go to the very bottom left and hit the Settings button.
3. Next, choose Grid type from the More Settings menu.
4. Choose the desired grid style.

Zoom In Or Out As Needed To Suit The Shot

1. Launch the Google Camera app.
2. Go to the very bottom left and hit the Settings button.
3. Pick a ratio that suits you:
   - Variety (16:9)
   - Wide view (4:3)

Resize An Image

1. Select the image you want to modify in the Photos app.
2. Select Crop from the Edit menu.
3. Feel free to resize the borders as you want.

Alter A Photo's Hue, Saturation, And Blurring

By way of the Photos app:

1. Locate the picture you want to modify.
2. Select Tools from the Edit menu.
3. You may change the saturation, hue, and blur of an image right here.

Image Sharpening

Important: Any Pixel device, including the Pixel Fold, running Android 7 or later may access this function.

Using Photo Unblur, you can fix your hazy images.

1. Launch the Photos app on your device.
2. Pick the picture you want to change.
3. Go to Tools > Edit picture > Unblur.

Hint: You may use Photo Unblur on both recent and archived photographs.

Pop

Note: Only Pixel 4a (5G) and newer models support this functionality.

1. Press Edit Picture, then Tools, and finally Pop in the Google Photos app.
2. Next, you may tweak the slider for scale.

Color Pop

Note: This function is compatible with Pixel 4a and older models.

1. To apply Color Pop to an image in the Google Photos app, go to the Photos tab, then press Edit.
2. Next, tweak the color pop slider to your liking.

Portrait Light

Important: Pixel 6 and subsequent models, including the Pixel Fold, are the only ones that include the Portrait light, Balance light, and Add light functions.

If you take pictures of people, you can change the lighting. When photographing close-ups of individuals or small groups, the best lighting for portraiture is from the waist up.

1. Press Edit Picture, then Tools, and finally Portrait Light in the Google Photos app.

- Select "Add light" to make the picture brighter.
- To direct more light to a certain area, drag the white ring.
- Turn down or turn up the light automatically or manually:
- Use the slider to personalize the brightness.
- Select Auto to allow your smartphone to control the lights.
- Press Balance Light to make shadows less harsh.

Lighten Or Darken As Needed.

Important: Note that this functionality is compatible with Pixel devices, including Pixel Fold, released after April 4, 2018.

Turn Up The Light: Slide the Brightness slider to the right to increase or decrease the brightness.

Adjust Shadows: Shadows may be raised or lowered using the slider on the right.

To Eliminate Or Reduce Interruptions, Use a Magic Eraser.

1. **Swipe up from the bottom of the screen.**

2. Tap the Camera app

3. Tap the Capture button

4. Select the thumbnail of the photo you just took.

5. At the bottom, tap Edit

6. Scroll through the menu to Tools.

7. Tap the Magic eraser.

8. There are a few ways to remove objects:
- Tap a suggestion
- Draw a circle or brush over an object to erase more distractions from the photo

9. When the object has been removed, tap Done.

10.   From here, you can continue editing, or tap Save copy to finish.

Note: Only Pixel 4a and later models use this capability.

1. Select the image you want to modify in the Photos app.
2. Press Edit, followed by Tools, and finally Magic Eraser.

3. Press a recommendation. You may remove more unwanted elements from the snapshot by using the circle or brush.
   a. Select Camouflage and then use the brush to make things disappear into the background.
4. Tap Done to conclude.

Get Rid Of Annoying Noises Using Audio Magic Eraser.

1. **Swipe up from the bottom of the screen.**

2. Open the Photos app

3. Select a video.

4. At the bottom, tap Edit

5. Tap Audio.

6. Tap Audio Eraser.

7. The audio will show up as a sound wave below the video. Your phone will identify sounds you can adjust in the video.

To edit the level of a sound, tap one of the categories.

Important: The result depends on the sounds in your video.

8. Drag the slider to the left to decrease the chosen sound.

9. Tap Play to check the new sound levels.

10. **When you're satisfied with the sound of your video, tap Save Copy.**

Note: You can only access this function on Pixel 8 and later models.

Use the Audio Magic Eraser app on your Pixel phone to remove distracting background noise from videos.

1. Launch the Google Photos mobile app.
2. To modify a video, tap on it.
3. Select Audio, then Audio Eraser, from the Edit menu at the bottom.
   - By selecting Auto, you may instruct your phone to make automatic adjustments to the volume.
   - By tapping on a sound and using the slider, you may manually alter the sound.
4. Select "Save copy" in the lower right corner.

Get The Shot In A Portrait Orientation.

1. Kick off your Google Camera app. Find out the steps.
2. Select Portrait, and then tap on Capture.
   - Tap the picture in the lower right corner to see the improved version.

Tip:

- After taking a picture, you may blur the backdrop by going to the Edit menu, then Tools, and finally Blur. To proceed, drag the Blur slider.

- The Pixel Tablet's front-facing camera is the only one that can capture portraits.

To Make Better Group Shots, Use the Best Take.

Note: You can only access this function on Pixel 8 and later models.

Best Take merges comparable group shots into a single shot so every person appears their best, even if someone in the shots isn't paying attention. Make your own Best Take by selecting your preferred expressions for each character.

To use Best Take for picture editing:

1. Launch the Google Photos mobile app.
2. Pick a picture to open from a series of related ones that include humans.
3. Find "Edit," "Tools," and "Best Take" toward the bottom of the screen.
4. You may change your expression by tapping on a face bubble.
5. After you're happy, hit the Done button.

Take Your Images To The Next Level With Magic Editor.

Note: Users must be 18 or older and have a Pixel 8 or later device to use this service. Because it is currently in its experimental phase, this feature may not always function properly.

Note:

- Android 8.0 or later, 4 GB of RAM and a 64-bit chipset are all requirements.
- Please be aware that this feature is still in its experimental phase and may not function as expected on all occasions.

Using contextual presets like "Sky" or "Golden Hour," you may reposition or remove portions of an image.

With Magic Editor, you can:

1. Launch the Photos app from Google on your Pixel smartphone.
2. To make changes to an image, just tap on it.
3. Press the Edit button, and then choose Magic Editor.

When using Magic Editor, to apply pre-made effects:

1. Press the Preset Edit Fix Auto button while you're in Magic Editor mode.

2. Get a default setting.
3. Simply swipe to the left to peruse your available choices.
4. Finish by tapping the checkbox.
5. To proceed with the picture editing, just repeat steps 1-3.
6. Select Save copy when you are through editing.

Tip: Notice that the preset choices are picture-specific. Not every choice is accessible instantly.

Use Magic Editor to crop, rotate, or delete an area of your photo:

1. In Magic Editor mode, you may choose an area of your picture by tapping, drawing a circle, or using the brush.
   - Focus closer for more precise results.
   - Simply touch and hold the area you wish to relocate, and then drag it to the desired location.
   - Hold down the selection with one finger and squeeze it with the other to enlarge or shrink it.
   - The Erase button will erase all of your choices.

2. Select the "Done" checkbox to save your changes.
3. Repetition of steps 1-2 will allow you to continue editing your shot.
4. Select Save copy when you are through editing.

Advice: Wait a few seconds for Magic Editor to make picture choices.

CHAPTER NINE

TIPS AND TRICKS

1. Generate Some AI Wallpapers

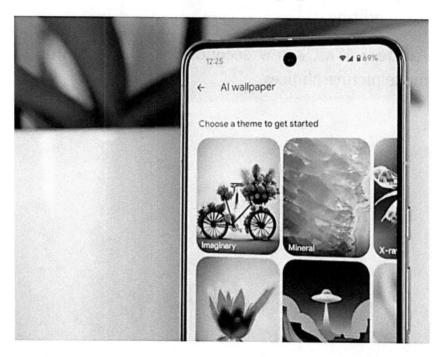

After making sure there are no updates, the second thing we do with almost all phones is add a personal touch. The simplest method to make your Pixel 8 unique is to change the wallpaper, but we'll get to some more customization choices soon. Wallpapers created by artificial intelligence (AI) are a powerful new feature in Android 14 that you may find interesting, however, you can always use a picture you've shot or a wallpaper you found on X.

Indeed, as long as you come up with creative methods to mix Google's prompts, there's no limit to how many backgrounds you may activate. Choosing this wallpaper is as simple as picking out any other:

1. The wallpaper option may be accessed by pressing on the home screen.
2. Pick out a design and wallpaper.
3. Explore more backgrounds by tapping on the option.
4. Opt for an AI wallpaper.
5. After choosing a category, you'll need to confirm your choices.

With Google's help, you can easily construct many possibilities using your enhanced Mad Lib responses; then, you can simply swipe between them to choose the one you like. Some of our own have already been created; you may see them here.

If you'd rather not tamper with artificial intelligence, we also have a plethora of fantastic themed wallpapers waiting for you to download on your Pixel 8. You may choose a screen that suits your taste, whether it's simple, nature-inspired, or gloomy.

2. Configure Face Unlock

Enabling Google's improved Face Unlock is another recommendation for Pixel devices powered by the Tensor G3. The Pixel 8 series has now attained Class 3 security, the highest on an Android phone, after pursuing Apple's gold standard, Face ID. This means that you can use it for mobile payments and purchases instead of merely unlocking your device. To keep the hardware to a minimum, the Pixel 8 series accomplishes its degree of security using smart machine learning algorithms, rather than adopting a larger infrared system like Apple does for Face ID.

If you haven't previously done so in the first moments of using your Pixel 8, here are the steps to take:

1. Go to the Settings option.
2. Please access the Security section.
3. Select "Face & Fingerprint Unlock" from the menu that appears.
4. You may access your biometrics by entering your PIN or passcode.
5. After you've followed the setup instructions, choose the Face Unlock option.

Having said that, Google's Face Unlock does have certain flaws. We suggest putting up a few fingerprints since it won't function in dimly lit environments or when you're wearing sunglasses or anything else that covers your face.

3. Customize Your Lock Screen

You may access the remaining personalization choices once you've fine-tuned your wallpaper using Google's generative AI. Changing the color of your clock and app icons has been an option with Material You for a while now, but with Android 14, there are a ton of additional clock styles to choose from. To complement the multicolored UFOs and canyon in my wallpaper up there, I went with a quirky lava lamp style, but you may choose from seven other ones. If that isn't enough, you have the option to disable or change the shortcuts in each corner. Getting to your lock screen settings is as easy as this:

1. Keep your finger on the home screen.
2. Wallpaper and style may be accessed.
3. Press the lock icon.
4. Alternate between different clock styles with a simple swipe.
5. Select an item from the list by tapping Shortcuts.

4. Turn On Now Playing

You may already be acquainted with Now Playing if you've ever used a Google Pixel smartphone. Should you not, it will undoubtedly become a beloved characteristic of yours. With Now Playing, the Google Assistant can now automatically recognize music, so you can say goodbye to Shazam. If you want to save yourself the trouble of memorizing every single song and band, just set your Pixel 8 or Pixel 8 Pro to listen. Here is how to enable Now Playing after the fact, in case you forgot to activate it while you were setting up your new Pixel device:

1. Go to the Settings option.
2. Just put "now playing" into the search box.
3. The switch must be turned on.

5. Use A Cover To Safeguard Your Pixel 8.

Back and front, the Pixel 8 series from Google are as sturdy as they have always been, thanks to a combination of aluminum and Gorilla Glass Victus. Still, it's not bulletproof; then again, neither is any phone. The display or back glass may still be cracked with enough drops and abuse, so it's important to be cautious. For this reason, you should splurge on a sturdy carrying case; to help you narrow down your options, we have selected a few of our favorites.

Fortunately, Google's Pixel 8 and Pixel 8 Pro users now have more case choices than ever before. You have two options: stick with Google's official case (although we want fabric back) or explore the vast world of third-party cases. others cases have carbon fiber, others include wallets, and still others, like Moment's, provide access to a plethora of additional camera accessories.